Andy Warhol

Paintings for Children

Prestel

A New Kid on the Block

Andy Warhol, whose real name was Andrew Warhola, was born on August 6, 1928 in Pittsburgh, a big city in the north east of the USA. A few years earlier, his parents had emigrated from Slovakia to America in search of a better life. Andy was the third of three sons. However, it took his mother a long time to feel at home in America as she didn't speak any English. Andy didn't learn English properly until he went to school.

As a child, Andy loved films more than anything else and collected autographs of film stars. Although his parents didn't have a lot of money, they still managed to give Andy a very special present—his very own film projector. He watched his favorite cartoons again and again, and in the end he started to draw, too.

Andy was only 13 when his father died, and it made him very sad. It also meant that no-one was earning any money, and so everyone had to help. Andy started to work, selling milk or fruit and vegetables.

Andy Warhol with his mother and elder brother John, around 1931

Warhol's high school graduation photo, 1945

'I never wanted to be a painter. ... I just wanted to be a tap dancer." Andy Warhol

Self-Portrait, 1942

Andy dreamed of becoming a tap dancer, a real star like the ones he had seen in films. This dream did not come true, but he continued to draw dancers and dance steps.

At school, Andy's teachers recognized his great talent for art, and gave him their support. He was allowed to go to art classes free of charge at a museum. And so he ended up studying drawing and painting instead of dance.

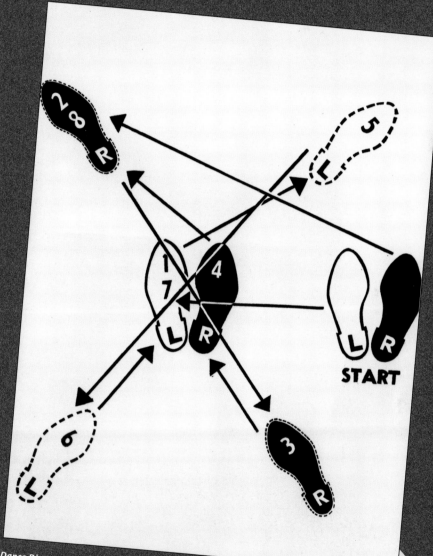

Dance Diagram, 1962

Here Andy Warhol has drawn some dance steps. Can you follow them?

New York, here I come!

Which shoe do you like best?

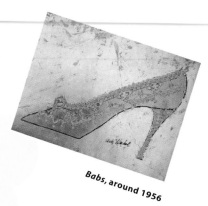

Babs, around 1956

After graduating, Andy Warhol went to New York with a big black art folder full of drawings under his arm. He went out looking for work and talked to the editor of a fashion magazine called "Glamour." Perhaps it was pure chance, but perhaps the name of the magazine attracted him—with its promise of magic, elegance, and beauty. Andy was given his first commission. He was asked to draw six shoes which were so magical that everyone wanted to buy them.

Andy drew shoes fit for a princess. Everyone thought his designs were wonderful, and he was asked to draw many more. He started to draw illustrations for fashion magazines, travel brochures, and art journals, and he designed record sleeves, book covers, Christmas cards, posters for window displays, and sets for fashion shows.

4

Above and right: 16 pages and the cover taken from the work *Search for the Missing Shoe*, 1955

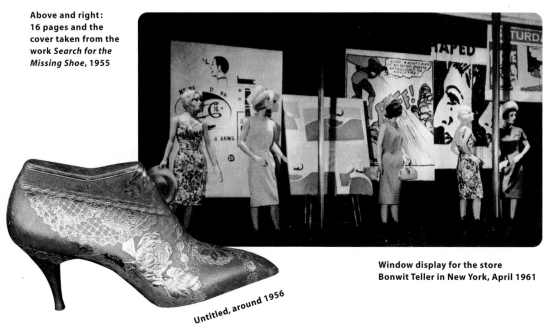

Untitled, around 1956

Window display for the store Bonwit Teller in New York, April 1961

Warhol at home with his mother, 1966

Andy's mother soon joined him in New York. At first they lived in an apartment where there was no hot water but masses of mice. As a result Andy had a lot of cats to chase them away. He called all the cats "Sam" and painted a whole book about them. He asked his mother to write the titles on his cat drawings, because he liked her old-fashioned writing so much. Sometimes she made a mistake, but that didn't matter to Andy because he didn't like everything to be perfect.

Sam, **illustration from** *25 cats named Sam*, **1954**

"Everything is beautiful" Andy Warhol

Coca Cola, tins of soup, stars and catastrophes

Superman, 1960

Eighty 2-Dollar Bills, front and back, 1962

It only took a few years for Andy Warhol to become one of the most successful and well paid graphic designers in New York. However, at the height of his success, he decided to do something different. He didn't want to work in advertising any more, or to draw expensive things. Instead, he decided to draw things that everyone can recognize and which are part of everyday city life. His first pictures were of comic figures such as Batman and Superman.

Then he drew things you can buy in supermarkets, like bottles of Coca Cola, tins of soup, boxes of washing powder, and even the money you use to pay for them.

Kellogg's Cornflakes Box, 1964

Campbell's Tomato Soup, 1968

Dollar sign, 1981

At the same time Andy Warhol started collecting illustrations from leaflets, newspapers, and magazines, which became starting points for his own art. He used photographs of flowers or snapshots of famous people, but also photos of sad things such as airplane crashes, car accidents, and race riots.

Can we call this art? Usually, art is something very special that no-one else can make. But Andy said: "I want to be like a machine," and he simply copied everything without changing it in any special way. This made a lot of people angry. They thought his pictures were scandalous, and soon everyone was talking about him. Andy Warhol was on the way to becoming a Pop art star.

Race Riot, 1964

POP!

Pop art is an international movement in painting, sculpture, and printmaking, which likes to show popular, everyday things in an exciting, explosive way

Andy Warhol at an exhibition of his flower pictures in the Ileana Sonnabend Gallery in Paris, 1965

Flowers, 1964

The Art Factory

Andy Warhol making a film in the sixties

Andy in the Factory, around 1964

Andy Warhol moved his art studio into an empty building which used to be a factory—so he called it just that. It became a factory for ideas and art, founded by Andy and his friends. In a way, it was still something of a factory because Andy no longer produced his pictures himself. Instead, he gave instructions to his workers. Quite often he didn't even paint—instead, he collected photos and made what are called silk screen prints. Instead of always trying out new ideas he used the same ones for years on end and produced the same series of pictures many times. Andy thought it was better to have hundreds of pictures rather than only one.

Andy tried his hand at other things, too. He bought a film camera and started to make films. He liked experimenting with dance, music, the spoken word, and film. What happens when you mix everything together? The Factory was not just an art studio but also a place to party. Artists, filmmakers, musicians, and all sorts of strange and interesting people met at the Factory. It felt like being in a disco because the walls were covered in silver aluminum foil or painted to look like metal.

When he was 39 years old, something dreadful happened: someone tried to kill Andy Warhol. A woman, who had acted in one of his films and who was mentally ill, shot at him three times with a revolver. Andy survived, but he never fully recovered.

It took four years before he started to paint again. And when he did, he painted pictures of skulls, pistols, and knives. It is clear that he was thinking a lot about his near escape from death.

Dead or Alive?

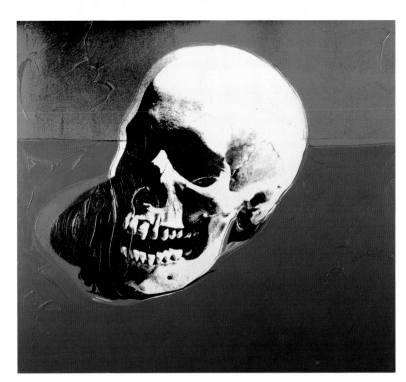

Skull, 1976

Mao, 1972

Knives, 1982

At the same time he started "painting" portraits. The first one was of Chairman Mao, the leader of the Communist revolution in China. One famous newspaper described Mao as the most famous person in the whole world. But actually, Andy Warhol painted portraits for anyone who had enough money to pay for one. Andy painted fifty to a hundred portraits a year until he died. It became very fashionable to have a portrait of yourself done by Andy Warhol.

Can pictures happen by chance?

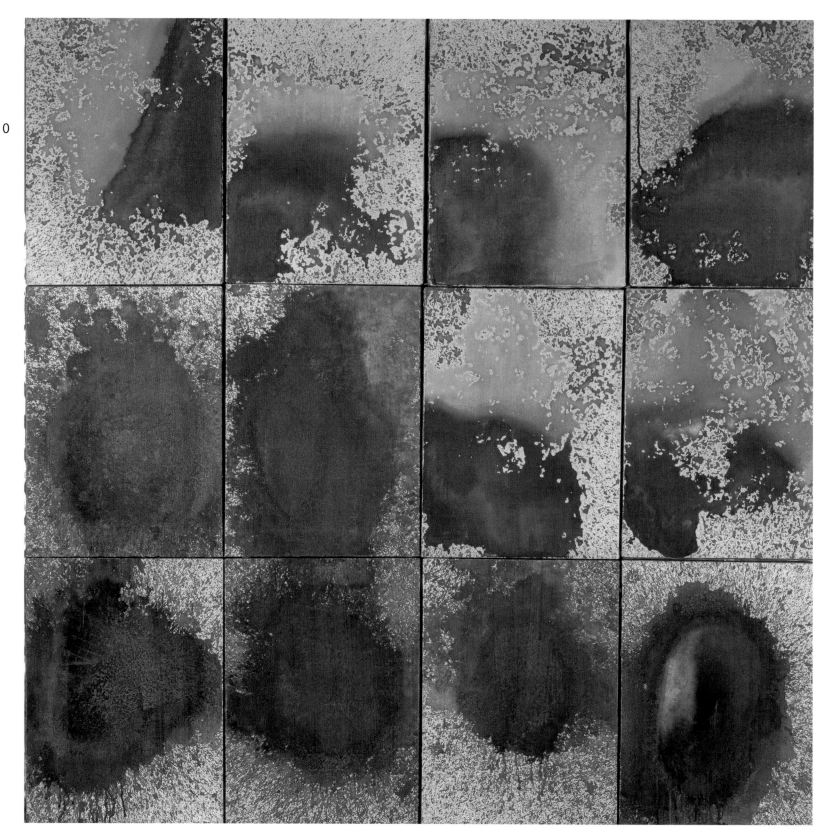

Oxidation painting, 1978

Sometimes, mysterious looking pictures can happen by chance, for example when you look at footprints in the sand, markings on a stone, or paint which has dripped onto a piece of paper. Many of Andy Warhol's artist friends made pictures in this way, dropping or spraying paint without knowing exactly where it was going to land.

Andy also made pictures like this, but he had a special way of doing it. First he painted his canvases with gold or copper paint. Then he dribbled liquid onto the surface while it was still wet. When copper gets wet, red and green patches appear. This is a chemical reaction called oxidization.

The liquid which Andy used was urine or "pee." This might sound a bit silly, but he may have been making fun of artists, who take their work far too seriously.

If you look at Andy's "oxidization pictures," you would never guess how he made them! They shine and shimmer beautifully like precious gold.

The back of the oxidation painting shown on the opposite page

When Warhol made these pictures, he didn't leave everything to chance. He didn't know what the plates would look like, but when he put them together to make one big picture, he arranged the plates carefully in a special order. Here on the back you can see that he noted exactly where each one should go.

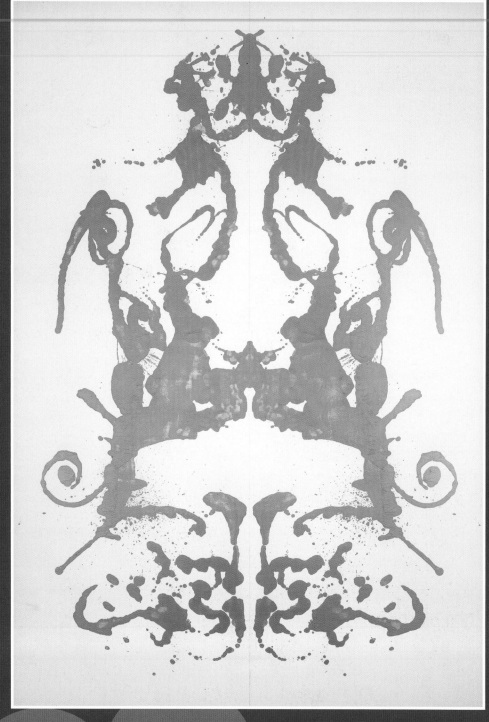

Rorschach, **1984**

Andy Warhol called the sort of paintings shown here "Rorschach" pictures. Rorschach was the name of a psychiatrist who asked his patients to look at pictures like these. They then told him what shapes or things they could see. He found that they saw lots of different things, and this stimulated their imagination.

The artist created a whole series of Rorschach pictures. He poured paint onto the canvas and then folded it in two. Usually, this sort of picture was quite small, but Warhol's "Rorschachs" are 6½ feet x 13 feet tall. Some are black, some are very colorful and look like butterflies, and others are bright gold.

Warhol said that he really wanted to employ someone to look at his pictures and tell him what shapes he could see. He thought this would make his pictures more interesting. But *you* could probably do this job for Andy just as well, don't you think?

I spy with my little eye, something which looks like a …

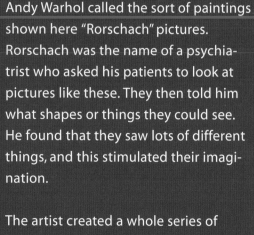

Have you ever tried anything like this? If you let drops of paint drip onto a piece of paper and then fold it, you can make wonderfully symmetrical patterns!

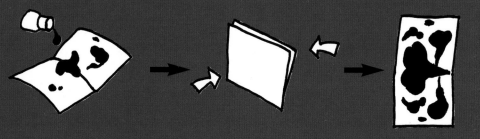

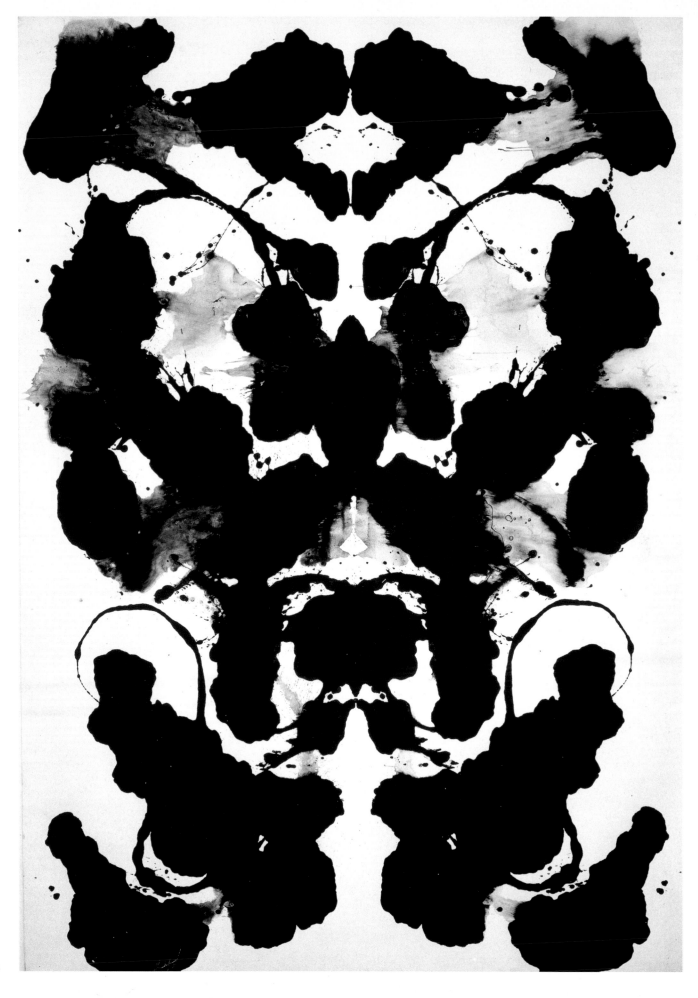

Rorschach, 1984

Light and Shade

Gold and silver were Andy Warhol's favorite colors. They make a painting look precious, but they are also very good at catching and reflecting light. Andy was fascinated by everything which shone and sparkled. Sometimes he scattered small grains of glass on top of his paintings so that they glittered like jewels. The name given to this glass is diamond dust.

One day, Andy had an idea. He wanted to make silver clouds dance around the room, so he filled large silver cushions with gas and put them in a draught. The result was an ever-changing picture of floating silver rectangles creating the sort of light and shade which you can often see in the sky.

When rays of sunshine break through the clouds, shadows become longer. The shape of the shadows depends on where the light comes from, and the light also changes the color of the sky and the earth. Andy Warhol painted more than 600 pictures of sunsets.

Although they all look similar, they are not the same. Warhol saw sunlight as a series of surfaces, and each time he used a different combination of colors. These pictures were not actually supposed to look like real sunsets—they were part of Andy's imagination. Have you ever seen a beautiful sunset? How many colors can you remember? Pink, violet, pale yellow….

Silver "clouds" in the Leo Castelli Gallery, New York, 1966

These pictures were not painted in the normal sense of the word. Andy Warhol used a special technique which allowed him to print the same thing many times in different colors. This is called silk screen printing because the picture is printed using a finely meshed piece of netting stretched tightly over a frame. To print something like a sunset, for example, you first have to cover up all bits of the netting where the picture is supposed to stay white. Then you cover the rest of the netting with the color you want and press it through the netting with a rubber scraper onto a white piece of paper lying underneath. The paint does not get though to the paper where areas of netting have been covered up. Uncovered areas let the paint through. You can also print photographs using a silk screen. For this you have to use a special sort of netting which can be exposed and developed like a photograph.

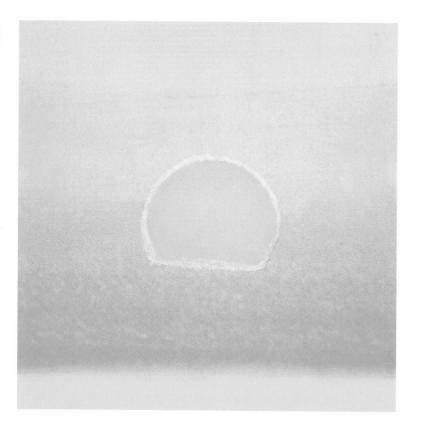 

Dog with Shadow, photo by Andy Warhol

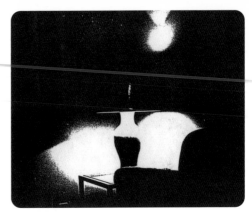

Lamp with Shadow, photo by Andy Warhol

One of Warhol's photos shows an armchair and a table with a lamp on it. The areas of light and dark are very clear-cut. The light from the lamp slices through the darkness and there are large areas of shadow. If you take bits from a photo like this and enlarge them, they look blurred and strange. But perhaps it is still just possible to see what object the shadow came from.

Like with his other series of pictures, Andy Warhol chose different color combinations when printing his shadow paintings.

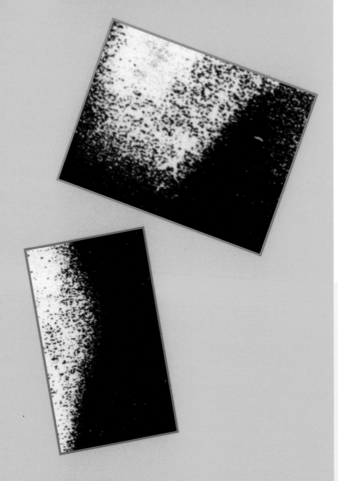

Andy Warhol liked playing around with light from different directions and discovering how it could affect shadows. He took photographs of the results,

and these were the starting point for pictures in which it is not possible to guess where the shadow comes from.

You can experiment with light and shade, too. Use a lamp to project the shadow of different things onto light-colored paper. When you move the lamp or the objects, the shadows change shape. You could draw round the outline of the shadows and color them in.

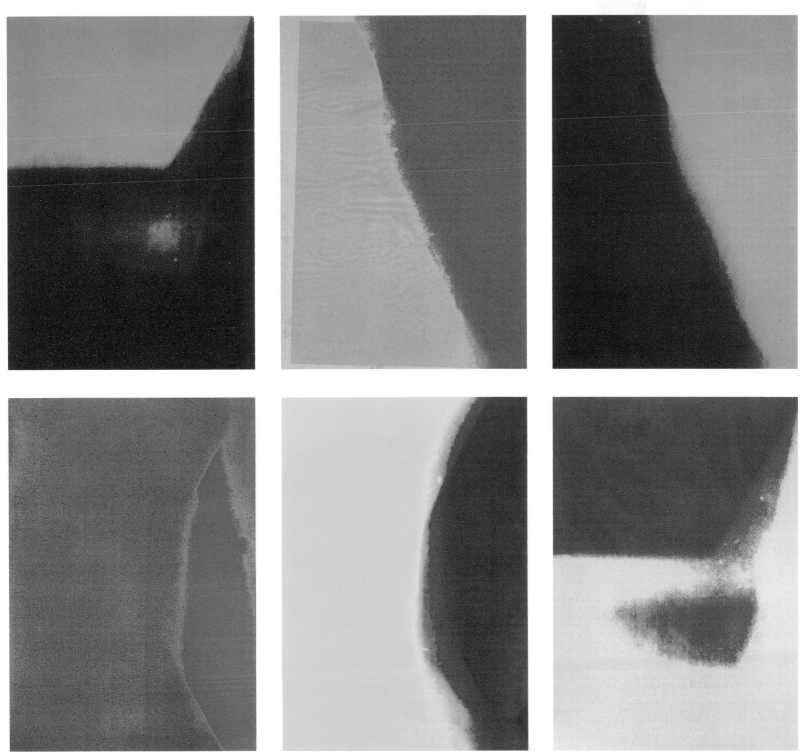

Six shadow pictures, 1979

Can you imagine what sort of things
these shadows belong to?

For children only!

18 Andy Warhol didn't have any children of his own, but he liked children and got along well with them. Perhaps one reason for this was because he loved collecting things, as children do, too. Andy had an enormous collection of toys and children's books from when he was young. He bought many of these things at flea markets or junk shops—such as a clockwork terrier which plays with a ball and a tin mouse which you can wind up.

When the Swiss art dealer Bruno Bischofberger suggested to Andy that he should hold an exhibition of pictures of children's toys, Andy was very enthusiastic and set to work. His own toy collection gave him lots of ideas. He chose small, simple toys like astronauts, clowns, monkeys, parrots, mice, fish, dogs, panda bears, airplanes, ships, and police cars. Each picture was printed several times in different colors, and each picture says what the toy is. Sometimes Andy also explained how it works, using the instructions on the box.

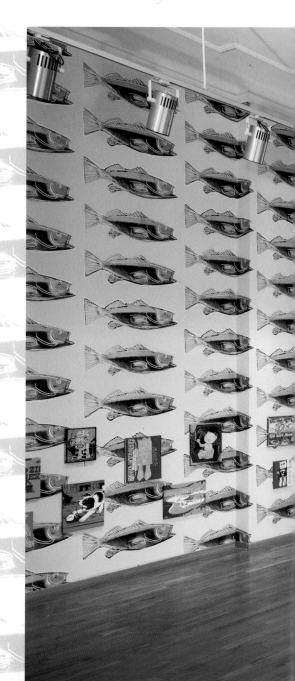

The exhibition "Pictures for Children" in the Bruno Bischofberger Gallery, Zurich, was opened on December 3, 1983

When the exhibition first opened, children were allowed to go in first. All of the pictures were hung low so that even the smallest child could have a good look. The grown-ups had to bend down to see. The walls were covered with wallpaper with fish on it, and visitors felt that they were walking through an aquarium! Lots of people came to see the exhibition, and it was a great success.

Here are the pictures of toys which were in the exhibition:
A ship, a fish, a scooter, an airplane, a panda, a parrot,
a moon explorer, another scooter ...

20

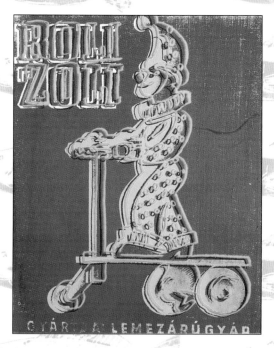

Andy Warhol's pictures of toys look like a small toy museum. What toys have you got? Perhaps you could make a few drawings of your own collection.

21

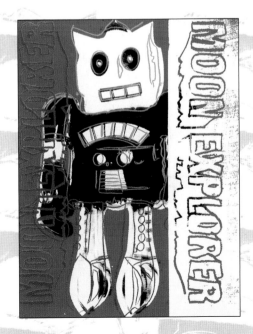

22

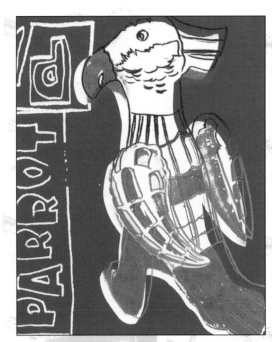

Time capsules,

and other attempts
to stop time ticking by

**Andy Warhol tried to capture
fleeting moments with his camera**

Andy Warhol loved collecting things. He didn't care if they were important or not, whether they cost a lot of money or next to nothing, or whether they were beautiful of ugly. He threw nothing away and always kept records. His collections reflect many of the things he had seen and done.

Nearly every weekend he went out shopping with a friend. They wandered through the shops, streets, and markets of New York looking for interesting things. He bought hundreds of biscuit tins, clocks, pieces of jewelry, and old furniture, works of art, blankets, baskets, Indian clothes, and statues, and in the end he brought home a whole pile of bric-a-brac. He had a five-story town house in New York, and whole rooms were full of the things he bought. Some were never unwrapped. A year after

Andy Warhol's death, more than 10,000 things belonging to him were sold at auction. This seems like an awful lot, but actually this was only a small part of his collection.

Andy also had an enormous collection of photos which he started as a child. When he was young he loved Shirley Temple, a little girl who was already a famous film star. He wrote a letter to her and she sent him her autograph. All his life he collected autographs of famous Hollywood film stars. He hoarded a huge number of photos from newspapers and magazines. Andy also kept thousands of his own photos, for he never went anywhere without his small camera. He wrote everything he did in his diary, and he carefully noted down everything he spent.

One day, Andy had a new idea; he wanted to put the steady stream of pictures and objects which passed through his hands into a sort of "time capsule." He took simple cardboard boxes and filled them with letters, documents, bills, magazines, snippets of paper, used cinema tickets, little presents, and souvenirs. Andy filled one box every month. Then it was taped up and put away. There was always a "time capsule" next to Andy's desk, ready for something to be thrown in. It was a bit like keeping a diary. By the time he died, Andy has filled 612 time capsules.

The kitchen in Andy Warhol's house

Warhol's diary, December 1962

One of Warhol's many "time capsules"

Would you like to make a **time capsule** too? You could make a birthday capsule, a holiday capsule or a winter capsule, and fill them with things which remind you of those times. What would you put in them?

The many faces of Andy Warhol

Andy Warhol was one of the most photographed people of his day. Even people who are not very interested in art have heard about him. He was a big media star. Not only did he have his own cable television shows together with other famous personalities, but he also took part in various advertising broadcasts and music video clips, and he acted in a popular television series. He also took part in fashion shows and posed as a photo model.

No other artist enjoyed so much publicity, and he was well aware of this. In a very clear-sighted manner he said: "I think I am a symbol of our times, of our culture, just as much as rockets and television."

Four self-portraits, 1966/67

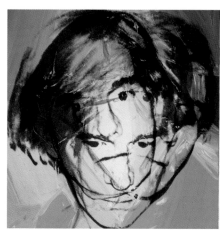
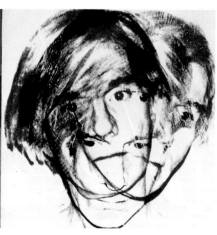

Self-Portrait, 1978

Section of wallpaper with self-portraits, 1978

Do you have a good photo of your face? You could photocopy it and enlarge it, and then use crayons and paint to make changes to it.

Here, Andy Warhol has changed the photo to his liking

Before and After 3, 1962

Andy Warhol was rather vain. As a young man, he had plastic surgery to shorten his nose and wore a hair piece. A few years later he replaced the hair piece with an eccentric silver wig. For him, it was quite normal that stars are in the habit of changing their appearance by using makeup, dying their hair, and wearing amazing clothes. With the right lighting and the right camera setting, they could then be presented to the public in the best possible way. Andy knew how to hold his head and hands to get the right sort of photo.

Photos form the base of many of his self-portraits. Photography is an art form which can present people as they wish to be, as opposed to who they really are. Photos can hide or change certain things which are not wanted. "I would rather remain an enigma," Andy announced. He hid behind his pictures. He imitated his favorite film stars, dressed as a woman or put layers of heavy white makeup all over his face so that it looked like a mask. In some of his self-portraits, he even put camouflage colors over his face. But none of these pictures show the real Andy Warhol.

Self-Portrait, 1986

Self-Portrait, 1986

Camouflage Self-Portrait, 1986

The Last Supper

The Last Supper (black/orange), 1986

Warhol collected many prints of this painting, including photos, copies by other artists, and even a porcelain sculpture of the scene.

Religious pictures were part of Andy Warhol's upbringing. He came from a very religious family and attended church regularly as an adult. Every room in his parent's house had a religious picture hanging on the walls. His brother John says that there was a picture of the Last Supper hanging above the table in the kitchen. Andy's mother also kept a small print of the Last Supper in her prayer book.

The Last Supper is one of Andy Warhol's last works, and in a way he is saying goodbye. He died quite unexpectedly after an operation in New York on February 22, 1987.

Andy Warhol used a masterpiece by another artist as a base for a whole series of works. Some pictures in this series were nearly ten feet high and thirty-three feet wide. They show *The Last Supper,* one of the world's most famous paintings which Leonardo da Vinci painted directly onto the wall of a monastery refectory in Italy around 500 years ago. He painted Jesus and his disciples having their last meal together. Before starting on his own work of art,